Inside
SPORT

# FOOTBALL

**Clive Gifford**

First published in 2007 by Wayland

Copyright © Wayland 2007

Wayland
338 Euston Road
London NW1 3BH

Wayland Australia
Level 17/207 Kent Street
Sydney NSW 2000

Senior Editor: Jennifer Schofield
Designer: Rachel Hamdi and Holly Fulbrook
Illustrator: Ian Thompson and Holly Fulbrook
Picture Researcher: Clive Gifford
Proofreader: Patience Coster

Picture Acknowledgements:
cover, 16, 18 John MacDougall/AFP/Getty Images; 1, 33 Carl De Souza/AFP/Getty Images; 3, 28 John Peters/Manchester United/Getty Images; 4 Michael Urban/AFP/Getty Images; 5 Jeff Gross/Getty Images Sport; 6 Stringer/AFP/Getty Images; 7 Antonio Scorza/AFP/ Getty Images; 8 Maxim Marmur/AFP/Getty Images; 9 Junko Kimura/Getty Images Sport; 10 Abdelhak Senna/AFP/Getty Images; 11 Andreas Rentz/Bongarts/Getty Images; 12 Patrick Stolllarz/AFP/Getty Images; 13 Khaled Desouki/AFP/Getty Images; 15, 21 Adrian Dennis/ AFP/Getty Images; 17 Paul Ellis/AFP/Getty Images; 19 New Press/Getty Images Sport;  20 Paco Serinelli/AFP/Getty Images; 22 Alex Livesey/Getty Images Sport; 23 Mike Hewitt/ Getty Images Sport; 24 Vincenzo Pinto/AFP/Getty Images; 25 Paul Gillham/Getty Images Sport; 26 Jan Pitman/Bongarts/Getty Images; 27 Clive Mason/Getty Images Sport; 29 Andy Lyons/Getty Images Sport; 30 Sergei Supinsky/AFP/Getty Images; 31 Matthew  Peters/Manchester United/Getty; 32 Toshifumi Kitamura/AFP/Getty Images; 34 AFP/Getty Images; 35 Patrick Hertzog/AFP/Getty Images; 36 Issouf Sanogo/AFP/Getty Images; 37 Cameron Spencer/Getty Images Sport; 38 Oliver Lang/AFP/Getty Images; 39 Phil Cole/ Getty Images Sport; 40 Stuart Franklin/Getty Images Sport; 41 Lars Baron/Bongarts/Getty Images; 42 Ben Radford/Getty Images Sport; 43 Jonathan Ferry;Getty Images Sport; 44 left David Cannon/Getty Images Sport; 44 right Rick Stewart/Getty Images Sport; 45 Staff/AFP/Getty Images; 46 Hachette Children's Books.


CIP data
Gifford, Clive
   Football. - (Inside sport)
   1. Soccer - Juvenile literature
   I. Title
   796.3'34

ISBN: 978 0 7502 5249 2

Printed in China

Wayland is a division of Hachette Children's Books

# CONTENTS

# INTRODUCTION

At its heart, association football, also known as soccer, is an incredibly simple team game with players controlling a football around a pitch and trying to score goals. Football has grown into the most popular team sport in the world offering excitement, action, drama and controversy.

## All Over the World

Football is played in most countries and is hugely popular with women and girls as well as men and boys. The game's best teams have tended to come from South America and Europe. However, large numbers of Asian, African and North and Central American footballers now play at the highest level and their national teams have become highly competitive. In 2001, a survey by FIFA (short for the Fédération International de Football Association) estimated that 240 million people play football regularly. Players enjoy the game's athletic, fast-moving action, the opportunity for individual skills to sometimes shine, and the importance of working together as a team.

*Japan's Yuji Nakazawa and Croatia's Niko Kranjcar tussle for the ball during the 2006 World Cup.*

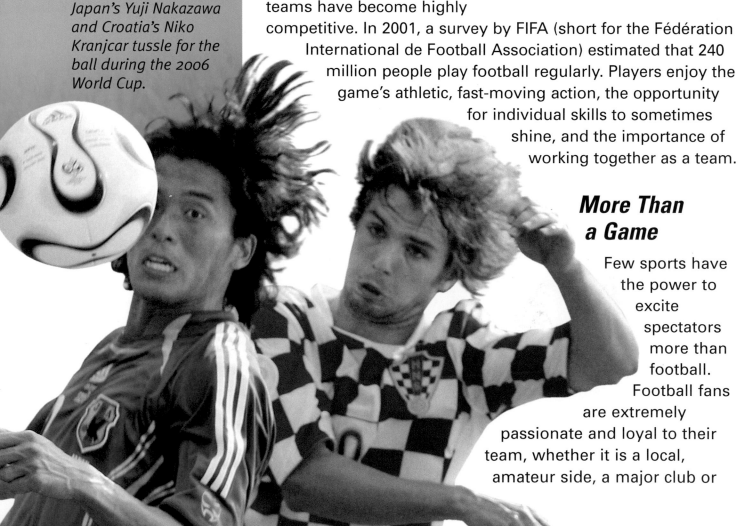

## More Than a Game

Few sports have the power to excite spectators more than football. Football fans are extremely passionate and loyal to their team, whether it is a local, amateur side, a major club or their country playing against other nations. In the top leagues, stadiums holding 70,000 or more fans are filled week in, week out, by supporters cheering on their teams, while whole nations are on the edge of their seats as their side competes in football's biggest competition, the FIFA World Cup. Over 600 million television viewers are believed to have tuned in to watch the 2006 World Cup final between Italy and France. The massive interest in football has turned top players into global superstars.

USA women's team star, Mia Hamm, chases the ball during a Women's World Cup 2003 match against Canada.

## STAT ATTACK

**Largest World Cup Attendance**

199,850 at the Maracana stadium in Brazil in 1950.

## Kitted Out

One of the reasons which helps to make football such a popular game is that it needs very little equipment to play – just a football and a pitch. Early footballs were made from a pig's bladder encased in leather which would soak up the water and become quite heavy. Modern balls are waterproof and lighter in weight; this helps players generate enormous speed in their shots or enables them to bend and swerve the ball in the air.

## MAD FACT

The first FIFA World Cup final in 1930 was played between Argentina and Uruguay. Both teams wanted to use their own football and in the end played a half each with their own ball.

A footballer's clothing is straightforward – shorts, a lightweight shirt, socks, and shinpads fitted inside the socks to protect the front of the legs. Soft leather football boots are fitted with studs or pimples on their soles to provide the right amount of grip for the pitch conditions. Today, top clubs and national teams make millions of pounds selling replica kits, just like the one their team wears, along with all sorts of other merchandise from casual clothing to jewellery. Italian club Fiorentina even sells three types of cans filled with air taken from their stadium!

# ⚽ FOOTBALL THEN AND NOW

There is no one starting point in the history of football. The Ancient Greeks, Arctic Inuit peoples and many others all had some sort of game involving kicking a roughly round object. Football grew out of various ball-kicking games in Britain in the nineteenth century and began to develop its own organized clubs and rules.

## In the Beginning

The very first football international was between Scotland and England in 1872. It ended in a 0-0 draw, although the rematch the following year saw England win 4-2. Both matches took place without some of the features of the modern game. For example, referees and pitch markings appeared only in 1891 and red and yellow cards were not used until the 1960s, around the same time as substitutes were allowed.

As the game grew in popularity, there was a need for organizations to run it. FIFA was formed in 1904 and is now the organization that controls world football. Its first World Cup was held in Uruguay in 1930. Each continent now has its own organizing body; in Europe, for example, it is UEFA. Each country has organizations that run leagues and cup competitions.

## Paid to Play

At the highest level of the game, it is impossible to separate football from the money in the game. Top clubs now earn vast amounts of money from television rights, ticket sales and merchandise, and spend much of their income on player transfers and huge wages. Until the 1950s, most footballers played for free,

**?**

### Who was...

#### ...Ferenc Puskás?

Ferenc Puskás was an extraordinary player in the 1950s and early 1960s. Short and squat, he possessed an incredibly powerful shot in his left foot, which saw him score over 80 international goals and an astonishing 511 goals in 533 games for clubs in Hungary and Spain. Puskas was a key part of the Hungarian team that went unbeaten for years in the 1950s. The team thrashed England twice (6-3 and 7-1).

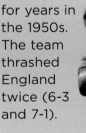

*Ferenc Puskás hits a trademark thumping shot with his powerful left foot.*

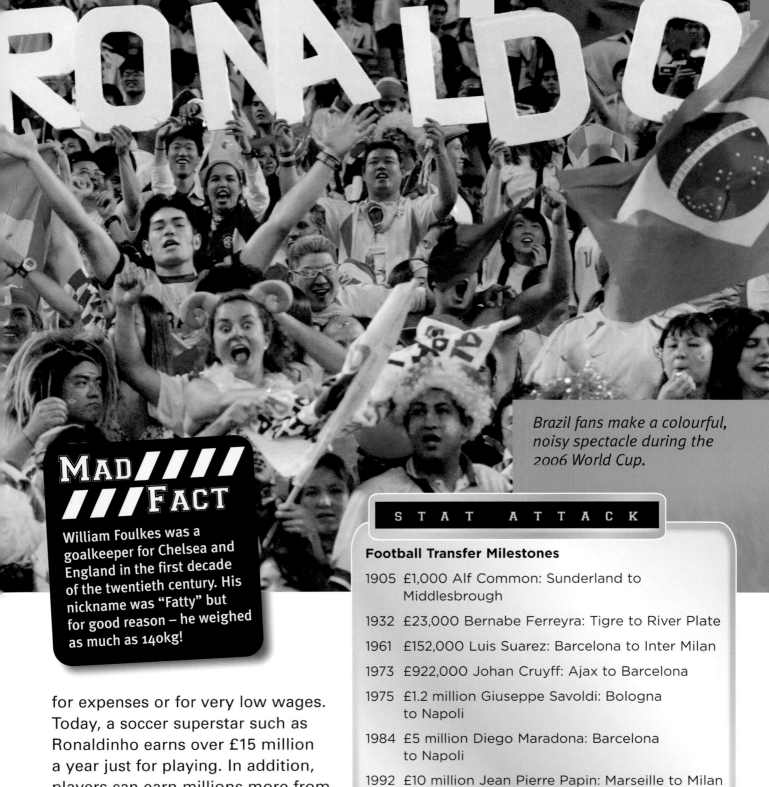

Brazil fans make a colourful, noisy spectacle during the 2006 World Cup.

## MAD FACT

William Foulkes was a goalkeeper for Chelsea and England in the first decade of the twentieth century. His nickname was "Fatty" but for good reason – he weighed as much as 140kg!

for expenses or for very low wages. Today, a soccer superstar such as Ronaldinho earns over £15 million a year just for playing. In addition, players can earn millions more from sponsorship and advertising deals with companies. In return, they train intensely, have to deal with the media and fans, and have all aspects of their diet and lifestyles monitored by their clubs.

## STAT ATTACK

**Football Transfer Milestones**

1905  £1,000 Alf Common: Sunderland to Middlesbrough

1932  £23,000 Bernabe Ferreyra: Tigre to River Plate

1961  £152,000 Luis Suarez: Barcelona to Inter Milan

1973  £922,000 Johan Cruyff: Ajax to Barcelona

1975  £1.2 million Giuseppe Savoldi: Bologna to Napoli

1984  £5 million Diego Maradona: Barcelona to Napoli

1992  £10 million Jean Pierre Papin: Marseille to Milan

1996  £15 million Alan Shearer: Blackburn to Newcastle

1998  £23 million Denilson: Sao Paulo to Barcelona

1999  £31 million Christian Vieri: Lazio to Inter Milan

2001  £46.9 million Zinedine Zidane: Juventus to Real Madrid

# AIM OF THE GAME

**Football is an eleven-a-side game with a simple aim –
scoring goals. The team with the most goals at the end
of the game wins.**

## *Game Time*

A full game of football is played over two halves of 45 minutes,
with a 15 minute long half-time period in between. A referee
decides how much time to add on for stoppages such as breaking
up a brawl or treating a serious injury. This added time is played
at the end of each half and at senior matches it is displayed on a
board by the fourth official. In some knockout competition matches,
such as the latter stages of the World Cup, teams that are
drawing at full-time play a period of extra or added time.
If the scoreline is still equal at the end of this, then a
penalty shootout (see page 33) is usually staged.

*Bayern Munich
midfielder, Mark
van Bommel uses
the side of his foot
to cushion a high
ball. With a
Russian Spartak
defender closing
in on him, he aims
to set the ball
down on the
ground
close to
his feet.*

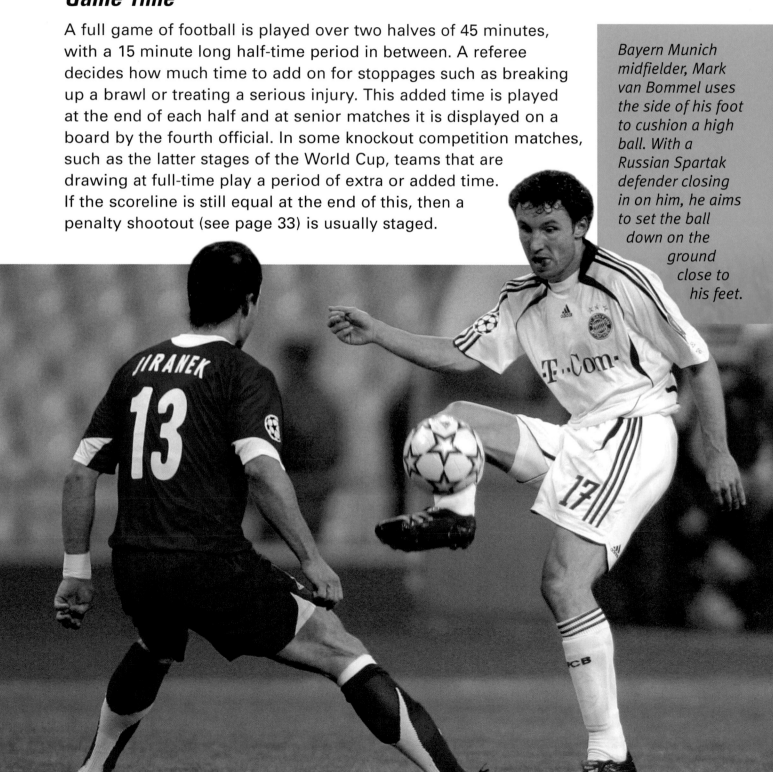

## Who is...

### ...Ronaldinho?

Ronaldinho Gaúcho is an incredibly skilful attacking Brazilian footballer. Playing his club football for Barcelona since 2003, Ronaldinho is a wonderful runner with the ball, able to weave past opposition defenders and make delicate passes or swerving free kicks. Voted on to the all-star team at the 2002 World Cup which Brazil won, he was also FIFA's World Player of the Year in 2004 and 2005 and the Champions League's 2005/06's most valuable player.

*Ronaldinho, playing for his club, Barcelona, hooks his foot around the ball to turn sharply. Top players have the ability to change pace and direction when they run with the ball in an attempt to beat opponents and set up a goal-scoring chance.*

## Goal!

In the middle of the ends of the pitch is the goal. It is made up of two posts 7.32m apart and is topped by a crossbar with its lower edge 2.44m off the ground. To score a goal, the ball has to pass through this rectangular box and completely cross the goal line. Judging whether the ball has completely crossed can sometimes cause debate. For example, one of Englang's goals in the 1966 World Cup final is still argued about today.

## Passing and Moving

Teams with the ball in their possession look to move it around the pitch, aiming to get close enough to their opponent's goal and in a good enough position to score. Players can use any part of their body to control and pass the ball, including their chest, head, feet and legs but not their arms or hands. A handball results in the referee awarding a free kick to the opposition or, if the player found guilty of handball was in his own penalty area (see page 14), a penalty. A football flies across a pitch so players need excellent skills to cushion and control a ball not just with their feet but also with their chest and thigh. When the ball is under a player's control, he can pass, shoot or run with it.

## Defending and Marking

The defending team strives to stop its opponents from scoring and also tries to rob them of possession of the ball. The team may try to tackle its opponents or pressure them into a mistake. Much of the time, defenders will mark an attacking opponent by standing close to him and between him and his own goal. Their aim is to move with the marked player, putting off the player with the ball from passing to him and denying the marked player the time and space to receive the ball and control it. Teams can mark individuals (known as man marking) or sometimes an area of space on the pitch (known as zonal marking).

# THE OFFICIALS

A football match is run by the referee and his two assistants who patrol the two sidelines. The assistants help to spot fouls, offsides (see page 11) and other infringements of the laws of the game. The referee's job is a tough one but without him, competitive games could not take place.

## A Referee's Role

A referee's work begins before a match when he has to assess the quality of the pitch, goals and goal nets and the general playing conditions. It is the referee who decides whether to call off a match because of bad weather, crowd trouble or anything else that could make a game unplayable. After a match, the referee has to hand in a report on the game. During a game, referees may run more than 9km to keep up with play. They have to make dozens of decisions under pressure, from deciding on who touched the ball last when it went out of play to whether to allow a goal or to rule one out.

The referee starts and stops the game using a whistle. He communicates his decisions to players using a range of signals. The referee's assistants indicate with their flags when the ball is out of play and whether a goal kick, corner or a throw-in should be awarded. They also use flag signals to indicate that a substitution is requested, a player is offside or whether offences have occurred out of the view of the referee.

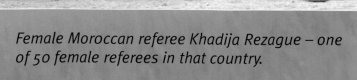

*Female Moroccan referee Khadija Rezague – one of 50 female referees in that country.*

## Playing Advantage

The referee must follow the laws of the game but he does have a little flexibility in choosing how he runs a match. For example, he may decide to talk to a player after a foul and warn him rather than book him (see page 13). He can also let play continue even if a foul was committed if, in his opinion, the team being fouled gains an advantage or benefits from the play going on. An example of this is if a player is fouled but still manages to pass to one of his strikers in a position to shoot. This is called the referee playing advantage.

## Offside

One of the referee's toughest jobs is to judge the offside law. In simple terms, a player is offside if he is in front of the ball when it is played, and is involved in play with fewer than two opponents between him and the opponent's goal. A player cannot be offside in his own half if he receives the ball directly from a goal-kick, corner or throw-in. A player who is offside will see a free kick awarded to his opponents.

Judging whether a player was behind the ball or two opponents at the moment the ball was played is extremely tricky and provokes controversy in many games. Sometimes an attacker has the ball and appears to be offside, but television replays show that he was not offside but timed his run forward extremely well. Referees also have to judge whether a player is involved in active play or not.

*Assistant referee, Jim Ouliaris, signals a foul by Germany's Mike Hanke on Mexico's Carlos Salcido. Playing in a 2005 Confederations Cup game, Hanke went on to receive a red card for the foul.*

# FOUL!

Football is designed to be a free-flowing game which stops only for a serious injury, when the ball goes out of play or when a foul or infringement occurs. Unfortunately, fouls and infringements, such as tripping an opponent, time-wasting or kicking the ball away at a free kick, happen all too frequently. The referee has to keep the game flowing and fair. He also decides what punishment to hand out to a player and his team.

## Free Kicks and Penalties

Referees award one of two types of free kick when a foul occurs: direct free kicks, where the ball can be kicked and scored from directly, and indirect free kicks where the ball must touch another player other than the free kick taker before it goes into the goal. Any offence worthy of a direct free kick becomes a penalty if the same offence occurs inside the offending player's own penalty area.

The different fouls that see direct free kicks awarded include: kicking, charging, holding or striking an opponent, spitting at an opponent and handling the ball deliberately. Indirect free kicks are given,

### STAT ATTACK

**Fouls and Cards at the 2006 World Cup**

**Most fouls committed:** 125: Germany, France

**Most fouls suffered (team):** 152: Italy

**Most fouls suffered (individual):** 23: Luca Toni (Italy) Luis Figo (Portugal), Cristiano Ronaldo (Portugal)

**Most yellow cards:** 24: Portugal

**Total yellow cards:** 327

**Yellow cards per game average:** 5.11

**Total red cards:** 28

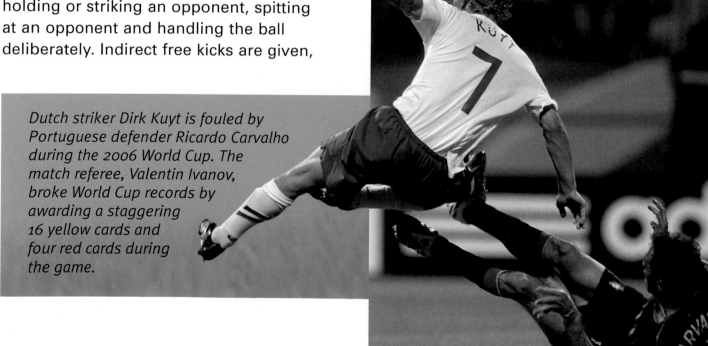

*Dutch striker Dirk Kuyt is fouled by Portuguese defender Ricardo Carvalho during the 2006 World Cup. The match referee, Valentin Ivanov, broke World Cup records by awarding a staggering 16 yellow cards and four red cards during the game.*

for example, when a goalkeeper breaks the backpass rule (see page 15), when the player unfairly stops an opponent's movement, by, for example obstruction, or when a player plays in a dangerous manner such as by raising his foot high and close to another player's head.

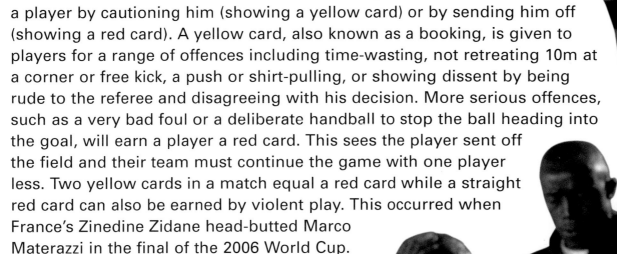

*Congo's Tresor Mputu (bottom) holds his head as the referee shows him a red card during an African Cup of Nations game.*

## Red and Yellow Cards

The referee can punish a player by cautioning him (showing a yellow card) or by sending him off (showing a red card). A yellow card, also known as a booking, is given to players for a range of offences including time-wasting, not retreating 10m at a corner or free kick, a push or shirt-pulling, or showing dissent by being rude to the referee and disagreeing with his decision. More serious offences, such as a very bad foul or a deliberate handball to stop the ball heading into the goal, will earn a player a red card. This sees the player sent off the field and their team must continue the game with one player less. Two yellow cards in a match equal a red card while a straight red card can also be earned by violent play. This occurred when France's Zinedine Zidane head-butted Marco Materazzi in the final of the 2006 World Cup.

## Simulation

At the highest level, the referee has his hands full, with players, for example, appealing for a corner or throw-in even though they know the ball came off them last. The most serious way of trying to cheat the referee is simulation. This is when a player pretends he has been fouled or seriously injured in the hope of winning a penalty or free kick or getting his opponent booked or sent off. Referees have to decide whether a player was genuinely fouled, or whether he has dived and is guilty of simulation which will result in the player receiving a yellow card.

# PEOPLE ON THE PITCH

striker

striker

left midfield

centre midfield

centre midfield

right midfield

left back

centre back

centre back

right back

goalkeeper

*A football pitch's markings and a typical line-up of a team, with one goalkeeper playing behind four defenders, four midfielders and two strikers.*

**Football is played on a pitch measuring around 100m long by 65–70m wide. Compared with some other sports, a football pitch has relatively simple markings. However, these are important as they are connected to many laws of the game.**

## The Pitch

Although artificial pitches are used in training and in some leagues, football tends to be played outdoors on grass. Muddy, water-logged pitches tend to be a thing of the past, at least at the top level, because pitch preparation is now an advanced science. Many pitches feature undersoil heating and artificial grass may be woven in with the real grass to add toughness. The grass used for the Sapporo Dome pitch in Japan at the 2002 World Cup was grown away from the stadium and moved there as an entire pitch.

## Pitch Markings

The pitch markings consist of the boundary lines – the sidelines and goal line – that mark out the edges, two pairs of boxes, the goal area and penalty area, and a halfway line and centre circle. At the middle of the centre circle is the centre spot from which each half of the game is started. It is also from where the game is

*Wayne Rooney waits in the technical area to come on as a substitute while the fourth official displays a board with the number of the player he is replacing.*

restarted after a goal is scored. No players from the opposing side are allowed inside the centre circle until the kick-off has been taken. A goalkeeper can handle the ball only inside his own penalty area. When the ball is passed back by foot deliberately by a defender, the keeper cannot handle the ball. If he does, the referee will award a free kick against him. This is known as the backpass rule.

## In and Out of Play

The ball is in play until the whole of it has crossed the sideline or goal line, along the ground or in the air. This is sometimes why you will see an official give a throw-in when a player bends the ball through the air down the sideline. Even if the ball's first bounce is on the pitch, it may have crossed the sideline completely in the air. When the ball goes over the sideline, the team that did not touch the ball last gets the throw-in. The same is the case when the ball goes out over the goal line. If the defending team touched it last, a corner is awarded to its opponents. If the team's opponents touched it last, the defending team gets a goal kick taken from inside the goal area. The one exception, of course, is if the ball crosses the line between the two goal posts and a goal is given.

## Substitutes

Substitutes are relatively new in football. They were allowed only by casual agreement in the past and first occurred at a World Cup in 1970. Today, teams are allowed to make up to three substitutions in each competitive game. In many competitions, the team's subs bench consists of five or seven players who may or may not include a goalkeeper. Players can be withdrawn from a match for a range of reasons, from suffering a slight or serious injury to underperforming; or a defender may be replaced by an attacker as one side chases the game.

## MAD FACT

At the 2002 World Cup, Cha Doo-Ri of South Korea came on as a substitute and was booked after just 20 seconds for a bad tackle. Bolivia's Marco Etcheverry holds the dubious record of being the substitute sent off fastest at a World Cup. In the 1994 game against Germany he received his marching orders after just three minutes!

# THE GOALKEEPER

The goalkeeper stands alone. As the player with the best view of how an opposition attack is developing, the keeper is expected to communicate instructions to his defenders and to command his penalty and goal area. A keeper's saves and skills can defend a side's lead or keep it in a game. A mistake by the keeper can lose the match.

## MAD FACT

Goalscoring goalkeepers are not as rare as many people think. German keeper, Hans-Jorg Butt has scored over 25 goals for his clubs, Hamburg and Bayer Leverkusen. His feats are eclipsed by Brazilian keeper Rogério Ceni, who has already scored 65 goals, mostly from expertly-taken free kicks.

## Agility and Bravery

Keepers train long and hard to become extremely agile and flexible. This enables them to leap high to collect the ball in a crowded penalty area or to dive wide to reach and deflect the ball around the goal post. Keepers also need great bravery to challenge for the ball such as by diving at the feet of an attacker. The backpass rule (see page 15) means that keepers cannot handle the ball directly from a throw-in or a kicked pass made by one of their team-mates. They have to use their head or feet to clear the ball.

## Awareness and Positioning

Much of a keeper's game is about avoiding having to make spectacular saves. Top goalkeepers such as the Italian, Gianluigi Buffon, or the Czech Republic's Petr Cech rely on superb awareness and reading of the game to position themselves in a way that makes a save look routine or easy.

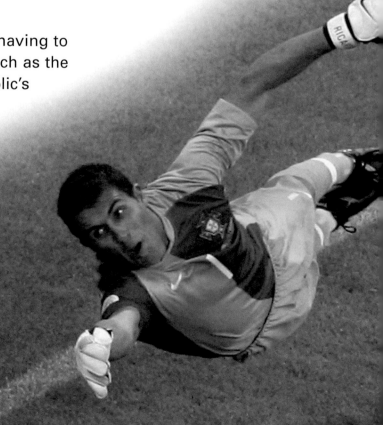

*A top goalkeeper like Ricardo of Portugal may not need to act for long periods but, when he is needed, he must react sharply.*

Behind a seemingly straightforward catch or a punch of the ball clear lie great concentration, fast footwork and good handling skills. Top keepers put in hours of training so that they learn how and where to position themselves. This includes knowing how to reduce the amount of goal space at which an opponent has to aim. They also work at placing their bodies behind the ball to act as a barrier.

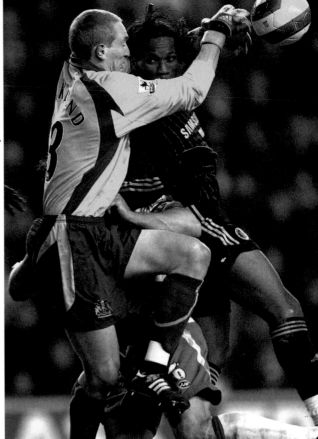

## STAT ATTACK

**Goalkeeping Records from the World Cup**

**Highest total number of clean sheets:** Fabien Barthez (France) and Peter Shilton (England) 10

**Most goals let in in total:** Antonio Carbajal (Mexico) 25

**Most goals let in in one World Cup:** Hong Duk-Yung (South Korea) 16

**Fewest goals let in by the champions:** Fabien Barthez (France) and Gianluigi Buffon (Italy) 2

*Chris Kirkland punches the ball clear. Keepers pride themselves on keeping a clean sheet – which is when their side does not concede a goal in a game.*

## Starting Attacks

A goalkeeper may be the last line of defence, but he can also be the first line of attack. When a keeper has the ball under control, he has six seconds to release it, otherwise the referee will award an indirect free kick to the opposition. In that time, the keeper has to choose where to move the ball to and in what way. This is known as distribution. The keeper can kick the ball from his hand, roll the ball out and kick it off the ground or use one of three types of throw – underarm, overarm or javelin – to distribute the ball. The underarm throw is the most accurate, the javelin often the quickest, and the overarm can be used for the greatest distance. Whether kicked or thrown, quick, accurate distribution can release a team-mate in space to start a useful attack.

In an 1894 FA Cup game between Preston North End and Reading, it rained so heavily that Preston goalkeeper, Jimmy Trainer played in a raincoat!

## Great Keepers

Top keepers lose few of their skills even into their thirties and some of the best keepers around have long careers at the highest level. In 2007, Oliver Kahn turned 37; David James, who had a great 2006/07 season with Portsmouth, was 36. Fabien Barthez retired in 2006 aged 36, and the great Dino Zoff was 40 years old when he captained Italy to win the 1980 World Cup.

# THE DEFENCE

A team's defence usually consists of three, four or five outfield players. These footballers work together as a unit to mark opponents. They also work with their other team-mates to repel the opposition's attacks and stop goals being scored against them.

## Jockeying

During a game, defenders will have many individual tasks to perform such as tackling, heading the ball clear and jockeying opponents with the ball. Jockeying is where a defender aims to get close to the opponent, with the ball to delay his progress so that other defenders can get into stronger positions. The jockeying defender tries to guide his opponent away from danger areas and, once there is support, may challenge for the ball with a tackle. When an opposing striker receives the ball with his back to goal, a defender may get closer. He tries to prevent his opponent turning to face goal and hopes to pressure him into making a mistake.

## Central Defenders

Strong and decisive both in the air and on the ground, a team's central defenders are the players most responsible for stopping opposition attacks breaking through the middle of the pitch. As many balls are hit long and high towards their goal, nearly all central defenders are skilled at winning the ball in the air and clearing the ball upfield and away from danger. On the ground, they have to be able to react quickly to opponents' turns and runs and may be forced into

**? Who is...**

**...Fabio Cannavaro?**

Fabio Cannavaro is a highly-skilled Italian defender who played for four Italian Serie A clubs before joining Real Madrid, in 2006. Famed for his superb anticipation and timing, which enable him to make clean tackles and interceptions frequently, Cannavaro has played 105 times for Italy and, as captain, lifted the 2006 World Cup. Although he is short for a central defender at 1.72m, Cannavaro is nonetheless extremely good in the air and was crowned FIFA's World Player of the Year in 2006.

*Cannavaro nudges the ball out of the path of Australia's Mark Viduka.*

18

a sliding tackle. The very best central defenders are also comfortable on the ball and can bring it out of defence, passing it to team-mates and linking defence and attack.

*Andrea Ranocchia tackles Alessandro Del Piero in a 2006 Serie B match. Ranocchia timed his tackle to put the ball out of play for a throw-in.*

## Full Backs

Full backs tend to be quicker and more mobile on the ground than central defenders, but they still need to be good in the air and able to make swift, clean tackles. They must mark and prevent opponents from playing wide. This includes stopping wingers from crossing the ball or getting past them and running with the ball into the penalty area. Full backs such as Germany's Philipp Lahm or England's Ashley Cole are fit, fast and possess a lot of stamina. They need stamina as they are expected to patrol most of their side of the pitch and be a link in attack by making a run along the touchline in front of their midfield to receive the ball. Full backs such as England's Gary Neville, France's Lillian Thuram and the Brazilian veteran, Cafu, are particularly skilled at this.

# THE MIDFIELDERS

Midfielders are often a team's most versatile players, able to both attack and defend well. They must possess large reserves of energy as they typically cover more ground in a game than any other player. A FIFA study of play in the 2002 World Cup revealed that a midfielder can run a distance of over 12km per match.

## Tracking and Tackling

Midfielders are always vital to a game. In many matches, the ball is in the middle of the pitch often, as both sides vie for possession. Midfielders need to be able to chase down the ball, win it in a tackle and then use it effectively. When their side does not have the ball, midfielders have to defend by tracking opponents. This means that they stay aware of and follow an opponent making an attacking run forward, trying to mark them out of the game. When their side has the ball, midfielders are often a vital part of an attack. Some players, such as England's Frank Lampard and Steven Gerrard, are renowned for making surging runs forward to get on the end of an attack and scoring with a powerful shot.

AC Milan team-mates Gennaro Gattuso and Andrea Pirlo. Both are midfielders, but Gattuso is more of a tough-tackling defensive midfielder while Pirlo uses the ball to make telling passes and keep attacks moving.

## MAD ////// FACT

With Luis Figo, Zinedine Zidane and David Beckham in their team, Real Madrid in 2003 and 2004 had the world's most expensive midfield with the three players' transfer fees costing £110 million!

## Anchors and Attackers

As the game of football has progressed, some central midfield positions have become highly specialized. Some teams, for example, play a midfield anchor. This is a hard-working, hard-tackling defensive midfielder who plays just in front of his defence. His job is to help protect his defence and break down the opposition's attacks. Other midfielders with superb vision and passing skills play a more attacking role, controlling play and looking for the pass that will give a team-mate a great scoring chance. These are midfield playmakers, such as Italy's Andrea Pirlo or Spain's Cesc Fabregas. Some particularly attacking midfielders, such as England's Paul Scholes, rising Argentinean star Lionel Messi or French legend, Michel Platini, play almost as an extra attacker just behind the strikers and set up goals or score themselves.

## Wide Midfielders and Wingers

Wide midfielders are expected to work hard to track their opposite number and provide lots of width in attack. Like David Beckham, they are expected to be excellent at crossing the ball from near the sideline into the penalty area. Wingers are a more highly-attacking version of the wide midfielder. They are players with the skills, pace and tricks to beat opponents and attack the opposition penalty area either with accurate crosses or by running with the ball themselves. Typical wingers were out of fashion for decades, but in recent times the supreme skills of players such as the Netherlands' Arjen Robben and Portugal's Cristiano Ronaldo have seen wingers back in fashion.

*Chelsea's Frank Lampard drives past Fulham's Michael Brown. Midfielders can dictate the play of their side by keeping the game moving, starting attacks and finishing them off with accurate shots and headers.*

## MAD //// FACT

In 1998 with a goal against Jamaica, Croatian midfielder, Robert Prosinecki, became the only player to score goals in the World Cup finals for two countries. In 1990 he had scored for Yugoslavia.

# STRIKERS

Strikers play a key role in their team's attacks and they are usually a side's most frequent goalscorers. In a tight match, a team's strikers may get only a handful of chances to score. They must take these and get their shot or header on target. A striker on top of his game can make the difference between a win and a draw or defeat.

## Different Types

Strikers come in all shapes and sizes, from relatively small players such as the great Argentinean Diego Maradona (1.66m) and Italian star Gianfranco Zola (1.67m) to tall target men like the Czech Republic's Jan Koller and Serbia's Nikola Zigic (both 2.02m tall). Strikers also play in quite different ways. Some strikers, such as the Ivory Coast's Didier Drogba, are strong in the air and good at keeping hold of the ball. These strikers often play as centre forwards, leading the attacking line and aiming to score from headers and through their power. Other strikers, such as France's Thierry Henry and Cameroon's Samuel Eto'o, rely on their pace, trickery and, sometimes, good passes from their team-mates to get behind the opposition defence or set up their team-mates in attack. Some strikers, such as the Dutchman Dirk Kuyt and England's Wayne Rooney, operate all over the pitch and may pop up on the wing or deep into midfield to receive the ball and run at opponents.

Liverpool's 1.67m-tall striker, Craig Bellamy is substituted in favour of Peter Crouch in their 2006 Champions League match against Maccabi Haifa. At 2.01m, Crouch is the tallest player in the English Premier League and the tallest to have represented England.

## Striking Skills

Possessing a strong, accurate shot, being good in the air and having an eye for goal are just three of the many attributes a striker needs to be successful. Strikers must have excellent vision and awareness of the game around them. They also need lightning-fast reactions to latch on to a loose ball from a rebound or to make a darting run into space. A good striker needs strength to hold off defenders as he controls the ball, and bravery to go in for a ball in a crowded penalty area with his head or foot. Just as importantly, strikers must have confidence to put a bad miss or a lean spell, where they have gone a number of games without scoring, behind them.

### Who is...

#### ...Samuel Eto'o?

Samuel Eto'o is a Cameroon striker who plays his club football for Barcelona. He scored 61 goals in his first 91 games. Fast, daring and with a devastating shot, at 18 Eto'o was the youngest player at the 1998 World Cup. Since then he has become the first player to be voted African footballer of the year for three years in a row (2003–05). He was instrumental in Barcelona's 2006 Champions League success and in 2005/06 became the first striker in the top Spanish league for 15 years to score 50 goals over two seasons.

## Defensive Duties

It may seem glamorous to be a striker but there is plenty of work apart from attacking for them to do. As part of the team, a striker has to be the first line of defence when his side loses the ball. He must chase and hassle the opposition defenders with the ball, closing them down and hoping to force them into a mistake or to intercept a pass. Strikers who are particularly good in the air often come back to help defend at corners and free kicks.

*Samuel Eto'o celebrates scoring the equalizing goal during the 2006 Champions League final against Arsenal.*

# TACTICS

The way a team lines up, the style of football it plays and the different moves and techniques it uses in attack and defence, are known as its tactics. The manager, or coach, is the person in charge of the team's tactics.

## The Manager's Role

Tactics are chosen according to the strengths and the weaknesses the manager believes exist in the opposition. For example, opponents whose defenders are large but slow might be best attacked with a number of fast forwards. Good tactics seek to use the skills of a team's best players to maximum advantage. For example, a team might support an in-form striker who is good in the air by playing wingers to deliver crosses to him.

Sometimes a dangerous opponent will be man-marked by one player throughout a match to prevent him getting the ball and scoring. The manager not only chooses a side's tactics but also chooses the players who will start the game. He decides on the timing of substitutes, if any, which can change the course of a match.

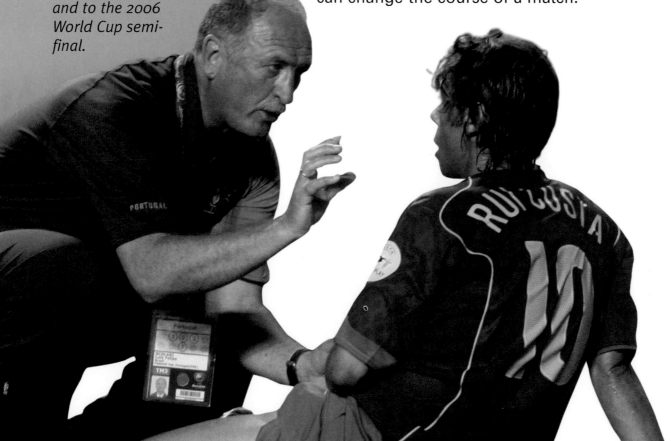

### MAD FACT

Juan Jose Tramutola was just 27 years old when he was head coach of Argentina at the 1930 World Cup.

*Phil Scolari (Luiz Felipe Scolari), manager of 2002 World Cup winners Brazil, also took Portugal to the Euro 2004 final and to the 2006 World Cup semi-final.*

## Formations

The way in which a team lines up at the start of the game is known as its formation. This is usually given as the number of defenders, midfielders and attackers lined up in banks across the pitch. For example, the common formation 4-4-2 consists of four defenders, four midfielders and two attackers. Many managers and coaches have tried a variety of formations, including 4-3-3 with a three-man midfield and one or two wingers linking with the strikers. Other teams may opt for a 5-3-2 formation, with a five-man defence with wing-backs (see below) or a 4-4-1-1 formation, with a striker operating behind another one. Italy played this latter formation on their way to winning the 2006 World Cup. Teams may often switch formations in a game, for example, changing from 4-4-2 to 3-4-3 by using their substitutes to bring on another attacker. Some teams protecting a lead in the last minutes of a game opt to bring on an extra defensive midfielder and may switch to a 4-5-1 formation.

### Managerial Statistics

**Longest-serving current top league manager:** Alex Ferguson (Manchester United) 1986–present, over 1,000 matches.

**Most World Cup matches as coach:** 25 Helmut Schon (Germany)

**Most international matches as coach:** 276, Bora Milutinovic (Costa Rica, China, USA, Mexico, Honduras, Nigeria)

**Most league titles at one club:** 18 William Struth (Glasgow Rangers)

**Winning World Cup as player and coach:** Franz Beckenbauer (Germany) 1974 as player and 1990 as coach. Mario Zagallo (Brazil) 1958 and 1962 as player, 1970 as coach

*Tottenham Hotspur's Aaron Lennon skips past the tackle of Manchester City's Kiki Musampa during an English Premier League game. Fast and fit, Lennon can play as a wide midfielder or he can be used as a wing-back, mixing defensive and attacking duties.*

## Wing-backs and Sweepers

There are also variations on the four-man defence. Some teams play a sweeper. This is an extra defender who covers the defence should an attack break through. Some sweepers play more of an attacking role, bringing the ball out of defence to become an extra player in midfield. A wing-back is a cross between a wide midfielder and a full back. Usually played as part of a 5-3-2 or 3-5-2 formation, these players need stamina to cover their side of the pitch in both defence and attack.

# PASSING AND MOVEMENT

**Passing the ball is the most important skill in football and helps a team to keep possession of the ball and build an attack. Passing must be accurate and at a height, speed and angle that the player receiving the pass can control easily.**

## Short and Long

A footballer can use different parts of his foot to propel the ball in different ways. The shortest but most accurate type of pass is when the inside of the foot (a sidefoot pass) is used to push or stroke the ball usually along the ground. For small flicks to the side, a player may use the outside of his foot, while for longer passes, he tends to use the instep of his foot – where his boot laces are. Whatever the length of the pass, it has to be hit with the right amount of force otherwise it might be intercepted by an opponent or might overrun the intended target or go out of play. If the receiver is moving, the pass has to be played ahead of him so that he can run on to the ball.

## Other Parts of the Body

In some situations a player can make a pass using another part of his body besides his foot. A cushioned header, for example, sees the ball headed gently so that it drops to a team-mate a few metres away. A flick-on header is played off the top of the head and is intended to pass the ball on to a team-mate behind. The chest can also be used to bring down a ball and leave it at that player's feet, or to deflect the ball or push it back to another player on the same team.

*Rising star Gareth Bale, looks at his target as he makes a sidefoot pass. He strokes through the middle of the ball to make it skim across the pitch.*

## Who is...

### ...Zinedine Zidane?

Zinedine Zidane was one of the most accomplished passers in world football. One of a small, elite group of players to win the World Cup (1998) as well as the European Championship (2000), Zidane was able to spot passes other players could not and could thread a pass through the tiniest of gaps.

He was also a terrific free kick taker, goalscorer and could run with the ball through defences. His last World Cup match before retiring, the final of the 2006 competition, was blighted by his sending off for head-butting Marco Materazzi, but Zidane was controversially voted the player of the tournament.

*Zinedine Zidane moves forward with the ball under control and his head up, looking for attacking options.*

**World Cup 2006 Crossing and Passing Statistics**

**Most short passes made:** Portugal 2,547, Germany 2,392

**Most long passes made:** Germany 821, Italy 711

**Most crosses made:** Germany 202, Portugal 166

## Movement

Passing works only if there are team-mates who are in good positions to pass to. To create space and time in which to receive a pass, a footballer has to move away from any opponent marking him and be in a good position to receive and control the ball.

One commonly used pass-and-move technique is the wall pass. Here one player passes to another, then sprints forward to receive a return pass. This pair of passes can cut out an opposition defender who is in the way.

Another classic skill is for a player to dummy, or pretend that he is going to run one way when, in fact, he cuts away and runs in a different direction.

# INDIVIDUAL SKILLS

Passing and movement are crucial individual skills for footballers but there are other skills, too, that footballers need, including heading, dribbling and tackling. A player must also learn to protect the ball by shielding it with his body and keeping his body between the ball and the opponent.

## Tackling

Tackles can be made from the front, the side or even from the back. In every case, the tackler has to be extremely careful to get the ball, to avoid fouling his opponent and to time his challenge perfectly. A fraction too early or too late and he may foul his opponent or his opponent may run away with the ball. The tackler's ideal aim is to win possession and move away with the ball. When this is not possible, he will try to prod the ball away out of his opponent's reach.

## Heading

There is more than one type of header. An attacker aiming for goal needs to position himself above the ball so that he can aim the header downwards. A defensive clearance header tends to be aimed higher and with plenty of power to propel the ball as far away as possible. Many headers are made under pressure from an opponent, so players try to time their leap to meet the ball at the highest point possible.

*Cristiano Ronaldo performs a drag back, where he pulls the ball back behind his standing leg to change direction.*

## Who is...

### ...Cristiano Ronaldo?

With bags of dribbling tricks, including stepovers and swerves, as well as pace to burn, Portuguese winger, Cristiano Ronaldo is one of the most exciting attacking talents in European football. After transferring from Porto to Manchester United as a teenager in 2003, Ronaldo has improved his game dramatically to become a lethal attacker and home-crowd favourite. He scored Manchester United's 1,000th Premier League goal in 2005 and reached a World Cup semi final and a European Championships final with Portugal.

MAD ///// FACT

England's 20-year old John Farnworth, a former Preston Town non-league player, won the World Freestyle Skills Championship in 2004. Farnworth also holds the world record for keeping a ball in the air just using headers for a staggering five hours, six minutes and 30 seconds!

## Dribbling

Dribbling involves moving with the ball and controlling it with a series of small kicks or taps. A straight dribble without any pace or variation can be easy to defend against. A good dribbler, therefore, adds various moves to his dribbling run, such as changes of pace and swerves, to make the dribble effective. A dummy and swerve move, for example, is where the dribbler threatens to move to one side of the defender by dropping his shoulder. When the defender begins to move in that direction, the dribbler swerves around him on the other side. Dribbling is a high-risk strategy but when performed in the opponents' half, it can sometimes lead to a goalscoring chance.

*Sweden's Anna Sjoestroem shows good strength and technique to shield the ball and hold off the challenge of Nigeria's Florence Iweta.*

# ⚽ SET PIECES

**Set pieces are devices by which the game is restarted after a foul, an infringement of the laws of the game or after the ball has gone out of play. Defenders need to be alert to the dangers; over 20 per cent of goals scored at the 1998 and 2002 World Cups, for example, were scored from set pieces such as corners and free kicks.**

*Shunsuke Nakamura takes one of his trademark swerving free kicks. The Japanese midfielder is one of the best free-kick takers around and scored a memorable 2006 goal for his club, Celtic versus Manchester United in the Champions League.*

## Corners

Corners offer a free cross deep into the penalty area. The player taking the corner may look for another player to flick the corner on to at the near post or may play a corner short to a player free on the edge of the penalty area. Central defenders' height and skill in the air often sees them come up the pitch at corners and free kicks. Corner-takers can bend the ball in towards goal or outwards, and a good corner is hit with pace, so that the slightest touch can deflect the ball towards the goal. Defenders try to mark up all their opponents in what can be a crowded area. They have to stay alert for last-second runs by attackers into their area.

## Free Kicks

Some free kicks close to a side's own goal, or in the middle of the pitch, may be taken quickly with the ball pushed forward or to the side to start an attack. Free kicks closer to the opponents' goal offer greater attacking opportunities. The defending team usually arranges a 'wall' which cannot be closer than 10m from the free kick. The attacking side has a number of options. A renowned swerver of the ball such as David Beckham, Ronaldinho or Juninho Pernambucano can bend the ball up and over or around the wall and towards goal. Alternatively, the team may play the ball to the side so that another player with a strong shot has a clear view of the goal.

**World Cup Shootouts**

There have been 20 games in World Cups decided by penalty shootouts since the first in 1982. The German team has won all four they were involved in, scoring 17 penalties. England has lost all three that they have been involved in, scoring only seven.

*Arsenal's Dutch striker, Robin van Persie takes a penalty against Charlton. Thierry Henry and the Charlton defenders look to follow up in case the ball is saved or rebounds off the post. They must not enter the penalty area until the taker has kicked the ball.*

# Penalties

Penalties are awarded for serious fouls or infringements inside a penalty area. The ball is placed just under 12m from the goal; a penalty kicked hard takes under half a second to reach the goal. A penalty is an excellent chance to score, but often the pressure becomes too much for some players who blast the ball high or wide or give the keeper the chance of a save. Keepers may move along their goal line before the kick is taken and can gamble on diving to one side or staying in the centre of the goal for a penalty aimed down the middle.

# Penalty Shootouts

A penalty shootout consists of a minimum of five penalties per side. It is the way many games are decided if they remain a draw after extra time has been played. Each team takes alternate penalties and, if the scores are level after the 10 penalties, pairs of players, one from each team, take penalties until one misses and one scores.

# GOAL !

**Goals win games. A team's tactics and attacking play must maximize the chances the side has to score. While free kicks and corners are important, the majority of goals are scored with the ball on the move in open play.**

## Who is...

### ...Pele?

Pele is the nickname of the Brazilian, Edson Arantes Di Nascimento, who was one of, if not the, greatest ever players in world football. A striker who played almost his entire career for Brazilian club, Santos, Pele scored over 1,250 goals for club and country and was part of three World Cup winning squads (1958, 1962 and 1970). Possessing astonishing vision and skills, as well as strength and pace, Pele was a true goal-scoring machine, scoring a hat-trick 93 times and notching four goals in a game a staggering 37 times.

*Top goalscorers like Pele react to situations quickly, try to get to the ball first and aim a shot out of reach of the goalkeeper.*

## Scoring Goals

Compared with other team sports, football is a low-scoring game. A single goal will often win a match. Teams may attack well, but without reliable players to put away the chances they create, they will struggle. Whether bursting through from midfield or playing upfront, good goalscorers have a natural eye for the goal and must be sharp and aware of the

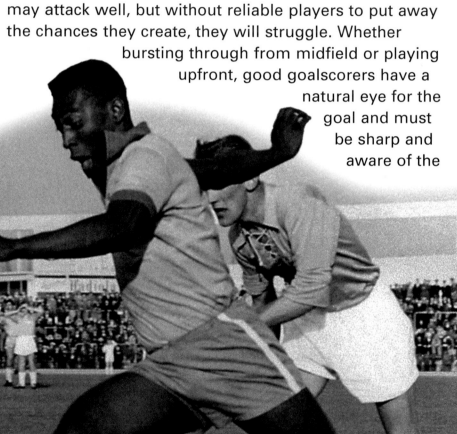

game around them. Occasionally, they will see a team-mate who is in a better position to score than they are and may attempt to pass the ball to him. However, most goalscorers take the chance themselves, reacting in an instant and choosing where to aim for and what sort of shot to use.

Some players are highly skilled at bending the ball and placing it in the upper or lower corners of the goal. Others opt for power and hit a drive with the instep of their boot, trying to keep the ball down and on target. In many situations inside the penalty area, the ball falls to a goalscorer who must react that instant. A high-bouncing ball may be hit goalwards by a diving header, a side volley or, if the player's back is to goal, an overhead kick.

## Stopping Shots

The defending team does its best to stop its opponents from getting a chance on goal. The team does this by dispossessing the player before he strikes, either by regaining possession, or, if under pressure, by clearing the ball away from danger. If their opponents get the chance to shoot, outfield players do their best to block the shot or header with any part of their bodies except their hands and arms. Now and then, a shot or cross hits a defender and deflects past the keeper to score an own goal.

*Italian defender Marco Materazzi leaps high during the 2006 World Cup final to score with a header. Central defenders are often good in the air and come up to attack their team's corners and free kicks.*

### STAT ATTACK

**Top Five Male International Goalscorers**

1. Ali Daei (Iran) 109 goals, 149 caps

2. Ferenc Puskás  (Hungary and Spain) 84 goals, 89 caps

3. Pele (Brazil) 77 goals, 92 caps

4. Sándor Kocsis  (Hungary) 75 goals, 68 caps

5. Bashar Abdullah (Kuwait) 74 goals, 132 caps

## Stirring Comebacks

Goals can turn games, so teams that are several goals behind strive not to give up but to double their efforts to score themselves. Pulling a goal back is crucial, as it can make the opposition defence jittery. It often leads to chances to score again. In the 2004/2005 Champions League final, for instance, Liverpool found themselves 3-0 down at half-time. They staged a stunning comeback to draw 3-3 with AC Milan and then succeeded in the penalty shootout that followed to win the competition.

# THE BIG COMPETITIONS

All professional footballers, whether they are up-and-coming young players or experienced veteran professionals, want to play in the biggest matches possible. Some of these are massive club games such as top-of-the league-clashes or the final of a cup competition. Other matches involve footballers playing for their country in international competitions.

## International Appearances

Representing their country is a major achievement for footballers. Many matches played by international teams are friendlies designed to test out a team and let the manager try out different combinations of players in his side. Serious matches involve qualifying for the World Cup and major continental competitions such as the European Championships, the Copa America or the African Cup of Nations. Many players, excellent at club level, fail to match their success at international level and manage only a handful of appearances, known as caps, for their country. Some star footballers manage to perform at the highest level for many years and notch up a lot of caps. Such star players include England's David Beckham (94 caps), Italy's Paolo Maldini (126 caps), Portugal's Luis Figo (127 caps) and Brazil's veteran defender, Cafu (145 caps).

**MAD FACT**

In January 2006, Kristine Lilly recorded her 300th cap for the United States women's team, an amazing feat. The world record holder for men is Saudi Arabian goalkeeper, Mohamed Al-Deayea, with 181 caps. Both are still playing.

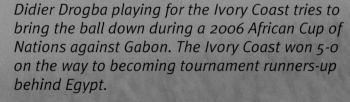

*Didier Drogba playing for the Ivory Coast tries to bring the ball down during a 2006 African Cup of Nations against Gabon. The Ivory Coast won 5-0 on the way to becoming tournament runners-up behind Egypt.*

## Continental Competitions

Each continent has some form of major competition which features the best national teams in the region. In Asia, there are two competitions, the Asian Cup and football at the Asian Games, an event which features other sports, too. South America's Copa America began in 1910 and is the oldest of the continental competitions. It has traditionally seen the powerful footballing nations of Argentina (14 wins), Uruguay (14 wins) and Brazil (7 wins) triumph, although in 2001 Colombia provided a shock by winning. Only three teams took part in the first African Cup of Nations. The 2006 competition was hotly contested by more than 40 national sides and the final was won by Egypt.

## Football at the Olympics

Football has appeared at the Summer Olympics officially since 1908, although tournaments connected to the Olympics were held in 1900 and 1904. For many years, it was a competition for amateur players but in the 1990s the rules were relaxed to include mainly young, professional players. At the 2004 Olympics, for example, the Portugal team included a young Cristiano Ronaldo. The 1996 Atlanta, USA Games marked the first gold medal for African football with Nigeria's Super Eagles; it also saw the arrival of women's football at the Olympics. The home team led by stars such as Kristine Lilly and Mia Hamm, won gold there and at the 2004 Athens Games.

### STAT ATTACK

**Recent Olympic Winners**

| Year | Men's | Women's |
| --- | --- | --- |
| 2004 | Argentina | USA |
| 2000 | Cameroon | Norway |
| 1996 | Nigeria | USA |
| 1992 | Spain | |
| 1988 | USSR | |
| 1984 | France | |
| 1980 | Czechoslovakia | |

*Australia's Tim Cahill makes a tackle on Bahrain's Faouzi Aaish during a qualifying game for the 2007 Asian Cup. In 2006, Australia left Oceania to join the Asian Football Confederation. This means that Australia now takes part in the Asian Cup and will also try to qualify for the World Cup from groups in Asia.*

# CLUB FOOTBALL

Clubs are the core of football. Players play for amateur clubs and lower-level teams, dreaming of a move to a big club playing in one of the major leagues. Most major leagues feature a pyramid system, with teams able to rise and fall between divisions of a league through promotion and relegation.

## The Big Leagues

Five leagues in Europe – Serie A in Italy, the Premier League in England, the Bundesliga in Germany, Spain's La Liga and France's Le Championnat – are considered the most important leagues in the world. Their clubs are extremely wealthy and able to attract top players from all over the world. For example, players from more than 75 countries from Algeria to Zimbabwe have played in the English Premier League. The top 50 most expensive player transfers have all been of players bought by clubs in those five leagues. Within each of these big leagues, there is a handful of bigger clubs whose buying power has enabled them to win many league championships. For example, in Spain, Real Madrid and Barcelona have won 36 league titles between them while in Italy, Juventus with 27 league titles, are Serie A's most successful side.

### STAT ATTACK

**Top Eight Average Attendances In Europe (2005–06)**

| | | |
|---|---|---|
| 1. | Barcelona | 73,225 |
| 2. | Borussia Dortmund | 72,625 |
| 3. | Real Madrid | 71,545 |
| 4. | Manchester United | 68,675 |
| 5. | Bayern Munich | 67,640 |
| 6. | Schalke 04 | 61,300 |
| 7. | AC Milan | 59,995 |
| 8. | Celtic | 58,150 |

*Bayern Munich midfielder, Lukas Podolski runs with the ball during the opening game of the 2006/07 Bundesliga season against Borussia Dortmund. Bayern Munich have been crowned Bundesliga champions seven times in the previous ten seasons.*

## Who is...

### ...Thierry Henry?

Thierry Henry is a French World Cup and European Championship winner who, after his £11 million move from Italian team, Juventus in 1999, has played all his club football for Arsenal. After taking ten matches to score his first goal, this lethal striker had been the top scorer for his club until 2006. He has become Arsenal's all-time leading goalscorer and at the start of 2007 had scored over 225 goals for the club.

*Arsenal's Thierry Henry lines up a shot as he is shadowed by Liverpool's Steven Gerrard during their 2007 FA Cup match. Arsenal has won the FA Cup a total of ten times.*

## Old and New

While some leagues have been running for a century or more, other countries have only recently introduced professional leagues. Japan's J-League began in 1993 and now has two divisions. Kashima Antlers, with 4 league titles, is its most successful side. Australia's A-League began in 2005 and features eight teams in a single league. In the United States, there has been a number of attempts to set up full-time professional leagues. WUSA, the women's professional league, was unfortunately stopped in 2003 but the male league, the MLS, has built a loyal following. In 2007, MLS side LA Galaxy announced a stunning swoop for David Beckham in a contract deal worth over £120 million.

## Cup Competitions

In addition to league football, almost all footballing nations have at least one cup competition that teams enter. The oldest and most famous club cup competition is the FA Cup in England. Held since the 1871/72 season, the FA Cup sees hundreds of amateur sides enter the preliminary rounds in August, hoping to get through round after round for a 3rd round tie against a Premier League team. Ten teams have won the FA Cup five times or more; up until 2007 Manchester United is the leading side with 11 wins.

# EUROPEAN COMPETITIONS

Whatever their nationality, many of the world's greatest players play for clubs in Europe. The continent is home of the world's richest clubs, such as Chelsea, Real Madrid, AC Milan, Bayern Munich and Manchester United. European club competitions pit most of the world's best players against one another. For the national sides of Europe, the European Championship is second only to the World Cup in importance.

## European Cups

There have been a number of cup competitions for European clubs including the Inter-Toto Cup, the European Cup Winners' Cup and the UEFA Cup. The European Cup, which began in 1956, was the most prestigious. Dominated at first by Real Madrid, who won an incredible five European Cups in a row, the competition saw the winners of national leagues play knockout pairs of matches, one at home, one away. The winner of each pair of games progressed to the next round. During the 1960s and 1970s, there were periods where teams won two or three European Cups in a row, but the 1980s was very competitive and saw teams from Eastern Europe win for the first time.

*Spanish striker, Raul plays for Real Madrid in the Champions League. With 54 goals at the start of 2007, Raul is the highest ever scorer in the Champions League.*

40

## Champions League

In the 1992/93 season, the European Cup was repackaged into a new format with small groups of teams playing one another in mini-leagues before entering home and away knockout games leading to the final. Despite criticisms of too many meaningless games, television rights have made the Champions League an incredibly wealthy competition to be a part of. A club that qualifies for the following season's competition by finishing high enough in its league can earn tens of millions of pounds. Teams from England, Italy, Spain, France, Portugal, Germany and the Netherlands have all won the Champions League, which has seen some epic games in recent years. These include Dynamo Kiev's 4-2 victory over Bayer Leverkusen and Barcelona's 2-1 win over Arsenal in the 2006 final.

Germany's Renate Lingor heads the ball away from Norway's Solveig Gulbrandsen during the Final of the Women's Euro 2005 tournament.

## European Championships

The idea of a tournament between the national teams of Europe had been around for half a century before the European Championships began in 1960. After experimenting with different formats, the tournament is now held once every four years, with 16 teams from the 50 or so that attempt to qualify. Euro 2004 was held in Portugal with the hosts reaching the final. They were beaten by Greece, the surprise team of the tournament.

## STAT ATTACK

### Women's European Championships Winners

| | |
|---|---|
| 2003-2005 | Germany |
| 1999-2001 | Germany |
| 1995-1997 | Germany |
| 1993-1995 | Germany |
| 1991-1993 | Norway |
| 1989-1991 | Germany |
| 1987-1989 | Germany |
| 1984-1987 | Norway |
| 1982-1984 | Sweden |

# THE WORLD CUP

The FIFA World Cup is the ultimate prize in football. From small beginnings, where 13 teams contested the 1930 competition, the tournament has grown to become the biggest single sporting event in the world. The 2006 World Cup's 64 games were watched live by 3.35 million spectators and an estimated cumulative television audience of over four billion.

## Qualification

The World Cup is held every four years and now has 32 of the world's best teams in the tournament, known as the finals. The qualification process begins several years in advance when around 200 footballing nations attempt to qualify to play in the finals. Qualifying can be tough and the fans of many major football nations are disappointed when their team does not make it through. Dutch fans, for instance, were distraught when their team failed to qualify for the 2002 tournament, while Portugal has appeared at only four of the 18 World Cups.

*Brazilian captain, Cafu, kisses the World Cup trophy after his side beat Germany 2-0 in the 2002 final. Brazil beat England, Belgium and Turkey in both the group and knockout stages, on the way to the final.*

### STAT ATTACK

**World Cup Winners**

**5** Brazil (1958, 1962, 1970, 1994, 2002)

**4** Italy (1934, 1938, 1982, 2006)

**3** Germany (1954, 1974, 1990)

**2** Argentina (1978, 1986)

**2** Uruguay (1930, 1950)

**1** France (1998)

**1** England (1966)

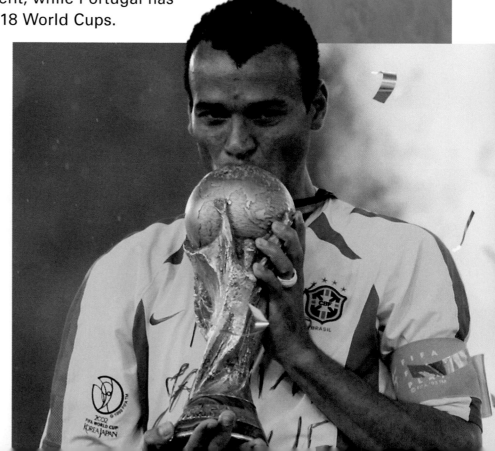

## Successful Sides

Teams from South America and Europe have won all the World Cup competitions. However, in in recent years, nations from elsewhere in the world have improved. South Korea reached the semi-final of the 2002 World Cup and there have been strong showings from Japan, Ghana, Australia and the USA. Only Brazil has appeared at all 18 tournaments and is the most successful World Cup nation with seven appearances in the final. Brazil has won five World Cups, and has the longest unbeaten run of 13 games between 1958 and 1966 and the longest run of wins – 11 at the 2002 and 2006 tournaments.

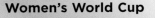

**Women's World Cup**

1991  USA 2-1 Norway

1995  Norway 2-0 Germany

1999  USA 0-0 China
      (5-4 pens.)

2003 Germany 2-1 Sweden

## MAD FACT

During the 1938 World Cup, Italy's Giuseppe Meazza was about to take a penalty when his shorts fell down. Coolly grasping the shorts with one hand, he scored the penalty which took Italy into the final which they won.

*Angola's Fabrice Akwa makes a spectacular overhead kick during the 2006 World Cup match against eventual semi-finalists, Portugal.*

## Scoring Feats

There have been many goals scored at the World Cup. In fact, it was not until 1958 at the Brazil versus England match that the World Cup tournament experienced a 0-0 draw. At the 2006 World Cup, Sweden's Marcus Allbäck scored the 2,000th World Cup goal. The player who scores the most goals at a World Cup is awarded the Golden Boot. Germany's Miroslav Klose, who scored five goals, won the 2006 Golden Boot. Brazil's Ronaldo won the 2002 Golden Boot and holds the record of most goals scored in World Cup finals – 15 in total.

Although in modern times, matches have become tighter but the occasional high-scoring game does occur. Costa Rica lost to Brazil in a 5-2 thriller in 2002 and followed it up at the 2006 World Cup with a 4-2 loss to the hosts, Germany, who had thrashed Saudi Arabia 8-0 in 2002. As the 2006 tournament progressed, games became much closer. Four games went to penalty shootouts that knocked out France, England, Argentina and Switzerland in the process.

# WORLD CUP LEGENDS

The sport of football has generated dozens of brilliant individual players, some of whom have been able to shine at the FIFA World Cup. Here are five players who have had a major impact on the tournament.

## Diego Maradona

Short, stocky but incredibly gifted, Maradona played at four World Cups. It was the 1986 tournament in which he really shone, as his amazing dribbling skills and eye for goal propelled an otherwise unremarkable Argentina side to win the World Cup. He then captained Argentina to the final of the 1990 competition, losing to Germany, before failing two drugs tests (1991, 1994) which saw the end of his international career.

## Ronaldo

A veteran of four World Cups and winner of two (1994, 2002), Ronaldo is a striker who, for a decade, was one of the most frequent scoring players in Europe.

He scored 47 goals in 49 games for Barcelona, 49 in 68 games for Inter Milan and almost 70 goals in his time at Real Madrid. Returning after serious injury, he was the top-scorer at the 2002 World Cup and holds the record for the most World Cup finals goals. With 62 goals for his country, he is Brazil's second highest goalscorer of all time.

**MAD FACT**

With a reputed age of 42, Cameroon striker Roger Milla, became the oldest player to both appear and score in a World Cup when he struck at the 1994 tournament.

## Just Fontaine

Frenchman, Just Fontaine played in only one World Cup, the 1958 tournament, but had a huge impact. He started the tournament out of the side, but injury to another attacker gave him his chance. He took it, scoring an amazing 13 goals in just six games. He still remains the highest goalscorer in a single World Cup. Injury in 1962 ended his career, by which time he had scored 165 goals in the French League in just 200 matches.

## Franz Beckenbauer

German footballer, Franz Beckenbauer played in three World Cups, reaching the final twice, and winning the 1974 tournament and the semi-final once. A stylish defender or midfielder, Beckenbauer was comfortable on the ball and turned the position of sweeper into a more attacking one, linking with midfield. He played almost 400 games for one club, Bayern Munich, and achieved 103 caps with the German national side. He later became manager of Germany and led them to victory in the 1990 World Cup.

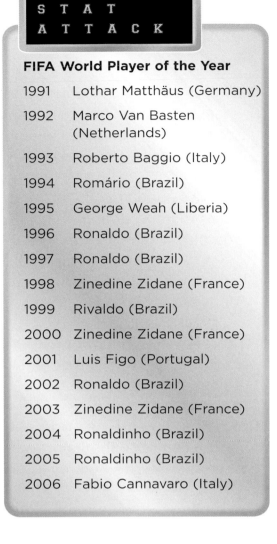

**STAT ATTACK**

### FIFA World Player of the Year

| | |
|---|---|
| 1991 | Lothar Matthäus (Germany) |
| 1992 | Marco Van Basten (Netherlands) |
| 1993 | Roberto Baggio (Italy) |
| 1994 | Romário (Brazil) |
| 1995 | George Weah (Liberia) |
| 1996 | Ronaldo (Brazil) |
| 1997 | Ronaldo (Brazil) |
| 1998 | Zinedine Zidane (France) |
| 1999 | Rivaldo (Brazil) |
| 2000 | Zinedine Zidane (France) |
| 2001 | Luis Figo (Portugal) |
| 2002 | Ronaldo (Brazil) |
| 2003 | Zinedine Zidane (France) |
| 2004 | Ronaldinho (Brazil) |
| 2005 | Ronaldinho (Brazil) |
| 2006 | Fabio Cannavaro (Italy) |

## Johann Cruyff

The key player in the great Netherlands teams of the 1970s, Johann Cruyff was an incredibly skilful and intelligent footballer. Technically a striker, Cruyff would pop up all over the pitch linking play, creating chances for team-mates and scoring crucial goals. His return of 33 goals in just 48 caps for the Netherlands would have been higher had it not been for his refusal to play at the 1978 World Cup. At club level, Cruyff was a major part of Dutch team Ajax's success as they won three European Cups in a row.

#  GLOSSARY

**Backpass rule** The rule in football which means that a deliberate pass backwards by a player to his goalkeeper cannot be handled by the keeper.

**Caps** The appearances for his national team in international matches that a top player may make.

**Clearance** Kicking or heading the ball out of defence.

**Counter-attack** When one team's attack breaks down and the other side starts to attack straight afterwards.

**Cross** Sending the ball from the sideline to the centre of the field, usually into the other team's penalty area.

**Cushioning** Slowing a ball down to control it by using a part of the body.

**Dummy** Pretending to move one way to trick an opponent but actually moving in another direction.

**Extra time** The time added on at the end of a football game when the score is tied at the end of full time.

**FIFA** Stands for the Fédération Internationale de Football Association, the international governing body of football.

**Formation** The way in which a team lines up on the pitch. The formation is usually given in numbers of defenders, midfielders and strikers, for example 4-4-2.

**Friendlies** International or club games played outside of a full competition.

**Handball** The illegal use of the hand or arm by a player.

**Hat-trick** To score three goals in a game.

**Instep** The part of the boot where the laces are.

**Intercept** When one team tries to pass the ball and an opponent moves and obtains it.

**Jockeying** The skill of delaying an opponent with the ball.

**Man-marking** Where a defender guards an opponent to try to stop him getting the ball.

**Merchandise** Ranges of product, from badges to mugs and shirts sold by clubs to supporters.

**Outfield** A term that refers to all players on the pitch, other than the two goalkeepers.

**Overlap** To run outside and beyond a team-mate down the sides of the pitch in order to create space and a possible passing opportunity.

**Pens** The abbreviation used in scoring to show that the game was won on penalties.

**Stamina** The ability to maintain physical effort over long periods. All players require good levels of stamina to stay effective over an entire match.

**Substitution** When a player is replaced on the pitch by another, fresh player.

**UEFA** Stands for the Union of European Football Associations, the body that runs football in Europe.

**Volleying** When the ball is kicked while in mid-air and before it bounces.

**Zonal marking** When a defender marks an area of the pitch instead of marking a single opponent.

# WEBSITES

**WWW.FIFA.COM/EN/INDEX.HTML**
The official website for the organization that runs world football. The site includes news, features and lots of information on the World Cup.

**WWW.UEFA.COM**
The home page of the Union of European Football Associations. UEFA runs the European Championship and the Champions League.

**WWW.THEFA.COM**
The official website of the English Football Association. This website has news on the England national team and all the English clubs, leagues and FA Cup.

**WWW.SHEKICKS.NET**
An information-packed website with coverage on women's football.

**WWW.SOCCERLINKS.NET**
A brilliant website with links to nearly 1,000 football-related websites.

**WWW.BETTERSOCCERMOREFUN.COM**
A website full of great coaching tips and tactics.

**Note to parents and teachers:**

Every effort has been made by the publishers to ensure that these websites are suitable for children, that they are of the highest educational value, and that they contain no inappropriate or offensive material. However, because of the nature of the Internet, it is impossible to guarantee that the contents of these sites will not be altered. We strongly advise that Internet access is supervised by a responsible adult.

# INDEX